The Worship and the *Worshipper*

Venetta Bloomfield

ISBN 979-8-88685-835-8 (paperback)
ISBN 979-8-88685-836-5 (digital)

Copyright © 2023 by Venetta Bloomfield

All rights reserved. No part of this publication may be reproduced, distributed, or transmitted in any form or by any means, including photocopying, recording, or other electronic or mechanical methods without the prior written permission of the publisher. For permission requests, solicit the publisher via the address below.

Christian Faith Publishing
832 Park Avenue
Meadville, PA 16335
www.christianfaithpublishing.com

Printed in the United States of America

Acknowledgments

Bishop Stanley Murray, who encourages and prays for me
Mother Elaine Catterell, who prays with me
Deacon Lawrence, who recommends Christian Faith Publishing
Joshah Bloomfield, my son, who guides me through
Sanique Wright, my grand-daughter

Introduction

The Lord has laid it on my heart for a few years to write this book on praise and worship, but I kept telling myself that I can't. I tried over and over, but I kept putting it off. Nevertheless, because of my passion for the subject, it was always in my spirit to do so one day. I remember going to Bible school, and the urge kept coming to me forcefully, but I still continued to resist. I told myself that there was no way I can do this; I wouldn't even know how or where to begin. In addition to that, there were many negative voices around me, and with no one to encourage or assist, I kept this vision to myself.

I used my inadequacy as an excuse, knowing that I had never been to high school. I did not even finish my primary education. Being raised by my grandparents, who believed that once you can read a little, it is enough. After that, they expected us to get married and have children. All this time, I was yearning to further my education and begged them desperately to go to other classes, but there was no help. Consequently, I grew up with very low self-esteem, knowing that my full potential was not being maximized. Despite this, the Lord saved me and I became more mature through His words. By this time, I was surrounded by people who encouraged me. Just hearing the word of faith being ministered helps to pull me up from negativity, and this is where my mindset changed.

I remember a few years ago, my local church back home was asked to go on a forty-day chain fast, in which I participated. It was during this fasting that I started writing and putting these notes together. Throughout the years, with the help of God, I was able to attend a few Bible schools, such as Morris Cerullo School of Ministry, Ebenezer Bible Institute, and Vision International University. From my studies, I was able to achieve an associate's degree in biblical studies, and during that time, praise and worship were main parts of my focus. I was then able to see better possibilities for writing this book.

As the Bible says, "I can do all things through Christ who strengthens me." I genuinely love to worship the Lord. It melts my heart to the point of tears every time I worship. Worship is a big part of my walk with the Lord, and I also love to pray. A few years after receiving my degree, I was doing full-time pastoral work, so prayer naturally became a part of my lifestyle. This is an essential part of all pastors' lives, as we are expected and should be able to lead God's people in the right direction. After all, we are accountable to God for those He places in our hands.

I was running a small business from home and I always look forward to those days when no one is home so that I can be alone with the Lord. This is the time when I hasten to the place where God, my Savior, shows His face; a time when I can be all alone so I can pour out my heart to Him in prayer and worship without any interference. Someone once wrote a song that resonates with me, "There are days I like to be all alone with Christ my Lord when I can tell Him of my trouble all alone." I did not just tell Him about my troubles, though; I also made this time a time of intimacy with the Lord. I don't think that the children of God should only meet with Him to tell Him of their troubles.

Prayer should be a time when we pour out praise and worship in the presence of the Lord. We should also make this a time of communication when He speaks to us through His Word. Sometimes we are blessed to hear that still small voice, while other times it is a word straight from the throne room of God. I remember one day, I was offering up some hallelujah praise to the Lord, and His presence came in that room so strongly that I started trembling. I was taken to another realm, which was an experience that I will never forget. It is pretty hard to explain; one would have to experience it for themselves to truly understand and be able to relate. I felt like if I stretched out my hand, I could literally touch Him. Coming out of an experience like this, all I can say is that God is real.

I have visited many churches and groups that are great worshippers, probably much better than I am in worship. However, I think some of our churches definitely need help in this area, and that is just my honest opinion. I wish for every believer in Christ to have a great and exciting experience in worship services, but how can they know without someone telling them and seeing the actual difference it makes in a person's life? I pray that these words will be able to reach someone who desires to hear them and apply them accordingly. Here and now, I put my pen and paper down to humbly write this book. It is my desire that it will be a blessing to everyone who spends time reading this book and to impart the same to the body of Christ.

Over the years, I've had this burning desire to see the church of Jesus Christ move to another level in the area of obedience to His words, concerning praise and worship. Not just staying in our usual traditional way of worship by singing a few hymns. I know we have some beautiful hymns that reach the depths of our souls, but to be the true worshipper that God is seeking for, we must be open to some changes in our day-to-day walk with the Lord and in the way we worship, for we have a progressive level in our walk with the Lord. Paul said we should "grow in grace and in the knowledge of our Lord Jesus Christ," and now is the time when He is seeking for such persons to stand in this area of ministry than ever before, and so I present the theme: "The Worship and the Worshippers."

The book of Psalm is one of the greatest books of the Bible. It teaches us about thanksgiving, praise and worship. It was written by great Psalmists. David, one of the greatest, said in Psalm 95- as he called us to worship. "Oh come let us sing unto the Lord. Let us make a Joyful noise to the rock of our Salvation. Let us come into his presence with thanksgiving. Let us make a joyful noise to Him with songs of praise. The emphasis here is placed on the word **US**. He is calling us to worship; the highest form of praise. So let us raise the bar.

Let us look at the word *worship*. What is worship? One Bible dictionary gave this definition of worship, and I quote what it said. The word *worship* means "to bow down, to prostrate, to honor, to reverence, and to pay homage to a superior being." It also came from the Hebrew word *worthship* which means "how much you are worth to me." When given to God, it involves acknowledgment of divine perfection. Searching through the Bible dictionaries, there are stages of development in the Bible patriarchs' worship. It started with Adam and Eve in the area of obedience to God's command. He asked that they eat from every tree in the garden except for one. They failed Him by their disobedience. Once we are in disobedience, fellowship is broken. Therefore, there can be no worship. Secondly, the first example of sacrificial giving to God is found in the account of Cain and Abel, and let us remember, they were the two first sons that were born to earthly parents. They both brought an offering to the Lord, but Cain's offering was rejected, while Abel's offering was received. And let us bear in mind that giving is a form of worship.

One of the common views of why the sacrifice of Abel was accepted was that it was a blood sacrifice and it was his best, but the sacrifice of Cain came from the ground. Anything we are giving to God, life must be involved in it; it cannot be anything that is dead. He said, "If any man will come after Me, let him first deny himself, give up himself, take up his cross, and follow Me." We must become dead indeed to sin but alive unto God. God then tried in the covenant way of worship as he dealt with the Israelites in the wilderness. This story is a very long one, so let us look for a moment at a small portion in Exodus 19. After God previously told the children of Israel not to have any other gods beside Him, nor should they bow down to any graven images, Moses went up to Mount Sinai to meet with the Lord for direction, and before he returned, the people asked Aaron for a god to help with their journey. This was also not enough. Even though building altars and offering sacrifices were a form of worship and worship is also an offering (Genesis 12:7–8), Cain and Abel offered two different types of offerings; one was received and the other rejected by God. Abel presented a more excellent sacrifice, which resulted in Cain killing his own brother. He himself said, after God asked him for his brother Abel, "Am I my brother's keeper?" When God handed down his punishment, he finally said, "I am driven out of your presence, for sin or disobedience separates us from God."

In the New Testament, true heartfelt worship begins when Jesus comes to earth. Through His life, death, burial, resurrection, ascension, and Pentecost, the believers now understood what Jesus had done for them. In response to this, they worshipped and preached like never before. The eyes of their understanding were opened. They now started walking according to the Word:

> The God we as gentiles can now declare "Thy word have I hid in my heart so that I might not sin against thee."

> But be ye doers of the word and not hearers only. (James 1:22)

> I will that men pray everywhere, lifting up holy hands, without fear and doubt. (1 Timothy 2:8)

> Speaking to yourselves in psalms and hymns, and spiritual songs, singing and making melodies in your heart to the Lord. (Ephesians 5:19)

> Then they that gladly receive the word were baptized and the same day there were added to the Church 3000 souls. (Acts 2:41)

> Upon the first day of the week let everyone lay by him in store. (1 Corinthians 16:1)

The above scriptures are talking about the early church coming together for divine worship. As souls are added to the church, and the spirit of the Lord is poured out upon the believers, they now become more mature and knowledgeable of the Word. And believing the Lord Jesus Christ to be the Messiah, in the spirit realm, things change. In the book of Colossians, Paul says, "The mystery which has been hid for ages and from generations is now made manifest to the saints by the spirit of the Lord." Jesus made mention in the book of John 4, that the Father is seeking for true worshipper who does not just draw to Him with their lips but their heart becomes involved. They should know why they worship and whom they worship. Now let us look through the divine Word of God into the life of a worshipper. I am not just talking about those that lead the worship in our local churches or on Sunday mornings, because every one of us as born-again believers is supposed to be worshippers.

I am praying that if no one receives anything from this book, those that stand in this area of ministry to lead the church of Jesus Christ in worship, both the singers and the musicians alike, will realize that this is an honorable possession that we are called upon to do and should be treated as such. There is a song that is being sung in many nations of the world, including mine. I am not sure who the writer of this song is, but if you will allow me to be a little critical here, I do not mean to hurt anyone. If it does happen, it is not my intention, but let me give my honest opinion on the words of this song. The words are, "Come just as you are to worship come just as you are before your God."

This is a beautiful song that we all enjoy, but I believe the writer was calling for the unsaved person that is not born again to come as they are to worship. As believers, the Bible clearly tells us how to come to Him. Please journey with me and let us see what the Bible has to say about worshippers. Under the old covenant in the tabernacle of Moses, if the priest went into the presence of God without cleansing himself, he would certainly die. In worship at the tabernacle, the high priest was set apart from all other men. He wore a special garment. It had to match the colors of the gate and the veil, which symbolize God's majesty and power, among other things. The garments were completed with a robe, tunic, sash, and a turban or hat. On the front of the turban was a golden plate, engraved with the words *Holy unto the Lord*, and there was a painstaking detail spelled out by God Himself to drive home the seriousness of sin.

The penalty was death, so a bell and a rope were attached to the skirt of his garment. As long as he was alive, the bell would make a noise, but if there was no noise, then they would know that he was dead. Due to this, they used the rope to pull him out because he went in unworthy. Let us look at three important areas in the tabernacle. The first one is called the outer court. This is the place where all the sacrificial lambs, goats, bullocks, and turtledoves were offered for the sins of the people. This ritual was done once a year, and each year, the priest had to offer a bullock for himself no less. Those sacrifices were without spots, wrinkles, or blemishes and were used as a symbol of the real sacrifice that was to come. The spotless Lamb of God, this sacrifice would be offered once and for all in the person of Jesus Christ.

The second essential area of the tabernacle is a basin filled with water that was in the middle of the tabernacle. For the priest to be considered cleaned he had to wash himself before he could go in to the holy place. Before he could speak with God on behalf of the people "For a clean hand a pure heart shall see God." This basin represents the laver of the Word. Jesus said in the book of John, "Father sanctify them through thy truth thy word is truth, this was a place of cleansing." The priest had to wash himself. "Let the Priest also which come before him Sanctifies themselves lest the Lord break forth upon them."

Similarly, in Leviticus 21:6, "They shall be holy unto their God and not profane the name of their God, for the offering of their God made by fire and bread of their God they do offer therefore they shall be Holy." Further reading, "Be ye clean that bear the vessels of the Lord, the Holy of Holiest is where the Priest come face to face with God. This is our possession in God for we are seated together in heavenly places with Christ Jesus, not just once per year like the priest but to dwell in his presence" (Isaiah 52:11). God's desire is that we come face-to-face with Him, but before we come, there must be a time of cleansing. In the case of an unsaved person who is coming for salvation, we can say to them, "Come as you are for the salvation of your soul."

Even the unbelievers must come to the Lord, according to the Word. They come, believing in their hearts that Jesus is the Son of God who came to redeem them from their sins. With their hearts, they believed, and with their mouths, confession was made unto salvation. Again, going back in the Old Testament, God called Moses at the age of eighty years old in the form of a burning bush. Moses drew near to see what the meaning of this bush that was burning without being consumed. The voice of God came out of the burning bush and said to Moses, "Take off thy shoes from off thy feet for the place where thou standing is holy ground." This is a holy place, Moses, so you have to put off some things. Remember, he murdered the Egyptian and hid him in the sand, and when he realized that it was known, he fled from Egypt. However, in obedience to God's demand after He dealt with him, he was now a ready vessel to bring His people out of Egypt.

Egypt is the very same place that he ran from, but God brought him back. Sometimes, from the same place that we fell, He will bring us right back to start over. God wanted to meet us face-to-face; He wanted to share His heart with us. However, before this happens, there must be preparation. From the beginning of time, God placed Adam and Eve in a very beautiful place called the garden of Eden, where everything was provided for them to enjoy, except for one fruit tree. God commanded them not to eat from it, but they disobeyed.

I believe the main reason God placed them there so that man would be in a place of fellowship with Him face-to-face. A true worshipper comes before the Lord in humility. Psalm 95:6 says that we should come bowing down before Him, but one day, He came for fellowship, and they were missing. Man disappeared from the presence of the Lord. He had to call for Adam. When he finally answered, he said he had found out that he was naked, and he hid himself. He was stripped from that righteous covering; he was no longer in this place of holiness, and notice what he said in Genesis 3:10: "I was ashamed and I hid myself." The Bible says in James 1:14 that we sin when we are drawn away by our own lust and entice, and sin when it is finished brings forth shame. Adam was ashamed; he was dead to righteousness, and he wasn't willing to repent. Instead of repenting, he blamed God for giving him the woman and said that the woman caused him to sin. The woman, in turn, blamed the serpent.

Let us, as worshippers, be like David, who said in Psalm, chapter 51, "It is against thee and thee only have I sinned and done this evil in thy sight, and then he asks for mercy and forgiveness." Let us remember that David was one of the greatest worshippers that ever existed, and even God described him as a man after his own heart because of his willingness to repent. God then drove Adam and his wife from their possessions. True worshippers must remain humble in the presence of the Lord. Let us also look at Isaiah 6:1. Isaiah said, "In the year that King Uzziah died, I saw the Lord high and lifted up." Who was this king that prevented the prophet from seeing the Lord?

During the years that this king was reigning, there was a long succession of ungodly kings and a dwindling of biblical faith, which spelled the downfall of Israel. They were ready to follow the example of pagan nations such as Asyria. They also look to them for protection and deliverance rather than on their covenant with God. I believe that during these years of this king's reign, all Isaiah saw was the wickedness of the kings, as they were God's leaders to the people. So Isaiah said, "In the very year that this king, Uzziah, died, I saw *also*, the Lord and He was high and lifted up."

It seems like the king was standing in the way of his vision so that he could not see the Lord. Is there any hindrance in our lives that will prevent us from seeing the Lord as He is? Is there anything blindfolding our eyes and limiting our vision of Him? Sometimes the way we look at the leaders of our country hinders our vision. We have so much dislike and hatred that we can never pray for them effectively, or the way we worship them takes the place of God.

When Isaiah saw God in His splendor and His glorious form, he said, "I saw the Lord. He is high and lifted up, the God that is high above all other gods and His train fill the temple." Remember now, the way we see God will reflect on the way we worship Him.

Isaiah realized there was room for no one else, and he could not go into the presence of the Lord the way he was. He cried unto the Lord, "Woe is me, for I am undone and I dwell among a people of unclean lips." Let us be open and honest with the Lord. He already knows everything about us.

God is light, and in Him there is no darkness at all. Therefore, in the light of His presence, sin is revealed or exposed, so it forces the person who desires to see the glory of God in worship to repent. Paul said, "I die daily; I make sure my body is under subjection." One may say that Isaiah saw himself in his unclean state. Yes, he did, but he could not remain in that glorious presence in an unclean state, so he prayed. After praying, the angel of the Lord flew straight to the man of God with a live coal in his hand, which he had taken from the altar. Look where he took it from; the altar, the place of fire, for fire sanctifies. Fire purifies, and the angel laid it upon his lips.

People's lips are considered their area of weakness. The angels then said, "Thine iniquity is purged thine iniquity is taken away and thy sin is purged." He immediately started seeing and hearing the voice of the Lord, and the Lord was seeking a vessel to be used. This was perfect timing, as Isaiah was now a ready vessel that could be used to shew forth the praises of Him who hath called him out of darkness into His marvelous light. The one who brought him out of his spiritual darkness and ignorance into the light of who he is.

As worshippers, we must know that worship is a response to the presence of the Lord. In worship, we joyfully embrace His dealings with us. The Bible said, "Great is the Lord and greatly to be praised." I will speak of the glorious honor of Thy majesty and of Thy marvelous works. God's presence will have a great and glorious impact on our lives flowing out of a relationship with Him. Our worship response is to offer our lives as a living sacrifice, holy and acceptable to God. This is our reasonable service in worship when the worshippers communicate with God, and therefore, we must spend time and energy in worship. The leaders must spend time in rehearsals and consecration before we come before God's people. One cannot lead people where they themselves have never been. Paul said, "Follow me as I follow Christ."

We spent a lot of time asking God for so many things. If we are not careful, every time that we meet with Him, it is to ask for things instead of spending time in worship. Often times in our church services, we can feel the Holy Spirit pulling us into worship, and because we have our activities planned for the day, we quench the Holy Spirit. Even the leaders are insensitive to the leading of the Holy Spirit, and we miss out on a move of God in the service. Sometimes all He wants is worship in our services. Let us remember that one move of the Holy Spirit answers for ten sermans and more.

We read that He inhabits the praises of His people, He lives in our praises, and He dwells in our praises. "What shall I render unto the lord for all his benefits toward me, or what shall I give in return for his blessings on me. I will take the cup of salvation and call upon the name of the Lord now in the presence of all his people" (Psalms 116:12–14). In verse 19, it says, "In the courts of the Lord's house, in the midst of thee o Jerusalem, praise ye the Lord." From our worship, we release words of knowledge and words of prophecy and healing takes place. The gift of the spirit will be in manifestation because strong worship opens the channel of communication between us and the Lord.

Due to this, prophecy will flow, and the presence of God will be so strong that the minister will be unable to minister the word. As recorded in 2 Chronicles, chapter 7, when King Solomon had finished praying at the dedication of the temple, fire came down from heaven and consumed the burnt offering sacrifices, and the glory of the Lord filled the temple. The priest could not enter the temple because the glory of the Lord filled it. The scripture further stated that when all the Israelites saw the glory and the fire above, they kneeled on the pavement with their faces to the ground, and worshipped, giving thanks to the Lord, saying, "He is good for His love and mercies endures forever."

This is what will happen when worshippers know who they are and whom they are worshipping. On the twelfth of December 2021, Sister Erica James said while leading worship in our local church worship service, "Your level of worship depends on your level of the understanding of who God is." I had to give a hallelujah shout in agreement with her words. I once read a little book on praise and worship where the writer said, "Worship is an excellent opportunity for the unsaved person to see the glory of God in manifestation, and by the worship they will be apprehended and convicted by the Holy Spirit." As worshippers, we must know that it is worship that plows and softens the soil of the heart for the seed of the Word to be sown in our hearts for us to become fruit bearers.

Worshippers must also know that it is by the offering up of intense worship that the hearers are more open to the Word. Another important scripture that the worshipper needs to understand is to be able to worship the Lord effectively. In John, chapter 4, Jesus met a Samaritan woman at a well and asked her for a drink of water, and she replied, "Sir, I have nothing to draw with, how can a person come to a well to draw water without anything to draw with?" However, as he built a conversation with the woman, it came to the area of worship, and the woman said to Jesus, "Our father worshipped in this mountain, and they told us that Jerusalem is the place where men ought to worship." This was bringing the woman into the tradition of men, and she was dedicated to the traditional teaching of her fore-fathers; however, this is the time when we need to move away from the way we worship traditionally.

Let's move away from our traditional worship and be led by the spirit, as Jesus said to the woman, "Believe me, the hour cometh when ye shall neither be on this mountain nor in Jerusalem to worship the Father." Notice that the woman was concerned about the place of worship. Jesus continues to say, "Ye worship and ye know not what you worship." In worship, we need to know who we are worshipping and why we are worshipping. If we don't, then we are just going through the rituals and format and the worship has no effect on our lives.

In many instances, we go to church dry and empty and leave it dry and empty. The Word reaches nowhere because the soil of the heart is not moistened. In worship, one cannot just know about God; we need to know Him. As I will be mentioning in this book over and over again, one must have a personal relationship with the Lord Jesus Christ to be able to offer effective worship. Jesus continued to say,

"The hour cometh, and now is that hour when the true worshippers shall worship the Father in spirit." The time is now to offer spiritual worship. We must bypass the flesh and give to the Lord true worship.

One that is set free by the truth of God's words, for it is the truth that makes us free, free from the bondages that hinder true worship. How can we worship in the spirit? One way to worship in the spirit, I believe, is to worship according to the word of the Lord Jesus. He said that His words are spirit and that they are life. Also, to be able to let worship flow from our spirit without being prompted by anyone. This will become a part of our lives so that we can't live without it. So when we get to church, there will be an overflow. Worship is an attitude of the heart; it is a celebration of the spirit to God in His supreme worth, and He said the Father is seeking for such worshipper. This is spirit-to-spirit worship. We cannot be in the flesh and offer this type of worship; we cannot walk in the flesh and offer this type of worship; we cannot walk contrary to the Word and offer this type of worship.

Jesus said that it is a must that we worship in the spirit. In Psalms, chapter 100, David says, "Come before His presence with singing and you must come knowing that the Lord is God. Enter His gates with thanksgiving and into His courts with praise. Be thankful to Him, and bless His name." As we said in the beginning of this book, we cannot just come as we are; there must Be a preparation before coming into His presence. What we must know, as worshippers, is who we are worshipping. To give effective worship, we must know who God is. Psalms chapter 95 says, "Oh come, let us sing unto the Lord. Let us make a joyful noise to the rock of our salvation. Let us come before His presence with thanksgiving and make a joyful noise unto Him with psalms, for the Lord is a great God and a great King above all gods.

He is above all other gods. The Scripture says that all the gods of the earth are silver and gold; they are the works of man's hands, but our God is the God that is great, Lord of all lords and King above all kings. The thing that makes me so excited is that I have been chosen to stay in the presence of this King to honor Him. 1 Peter 2:9 says, "For we are a chosen generation, a royal priesthood, a holy nation. A peculiar people call to show forth the praises of Him who hath called us out of darkness into His marvelous light." Hallelujah. Worship is a form of warfare, and in every warfare, we have to be armed with some weapons.

It is written in Ephesians, chapter 6, "Put on the whole armor of God that ye may be able to stand against the wiles of the devil for he is going about like a roaring lion seeking whom he may devour." This is one of the greatest weapons that is given to the church, and remember, I said one of because we have two other great weapons, which are prayer and the Word, among others, such as the blood and the name of Jesus. We are, however, only looking mostly at the weapon of worship. I will make mention of a psalm that has to do with two of these weapons, which are worship and the Word. Psalm 145 tells us to let the high praises of God be in our mouth; one of the great members of our body is our mouth.

The Word of God says that death and life are in the power of the tongue, which the mouth controls, and we shall have what we say, so we use it like a two-edged sword in our hand. The sword is the Word of God, and these weapons are used to execute vengeance. We execute punishment upon the people. We also use it to bind kings with chains and their nobles with fetters of iron. The Word is quick and powerful, sharper than any two-edged sword. It pierces the heart, and it is a discerner of the thoughts and the intent of the heart. And what do we execute? We use the divine Word of God and the written judgement of God to execute vengeance upon the heathen and punishment upon the people.

It is by the Word that we are judged and by the Word that we are condemned. But thanks be to God if our hearts condemn us. God is greater than our heart, for when we worship, we are supposed to use the Word. When we pray, we pray the Word. This honor belongs to all His saints, and every one of us is called to this honorable service. Psalms 85:11 says, "Teach me thy way oh Lord I will walk in thy truth, unite my heart to fear thy name the fear of the lord is the beginning of wisdom it perpell us to worship." He is Elohim, the Creator of heaven and earth; without Him, nothing was made; and His name is Jesus, the name above every name.

Psalms 96:3 says, "Declare his glory among the heathen, his wonders among all people why do we do this, for the Lord is great and greatly to be praised." He is to be feared above all gods. For all the gods of the nations are idols, but the Lord made the heavens. Honor and majesty are before Him; strength and beauty are in His sanctuary, so let us worship the Lord in the beauty of His holiness. He is Jehovah Mekadesh, the Lord our Savior; He is Jehovah Sabaoth—the Lord of hosts; Jehovah Rapha—the Lord our Healer; Adonai, the sovereign Lord; Jehovah Rohi, our shepherd; Jehovah Tsidkenu—our righteousness; Jehovah Jireh, my provider; Jehovah Shalom, He is our peace.

Why should we worship like never before? We have an opposition to our worship because he fell from the splendor of it and cannot return. Not only is he unable to return, but he desired this honor and was denied. Let us see what the Bible says about this enemy we are fighting against. Now the name Lucifer was given to Satan by God during his reign in heaven. The name Lucifer came from the Hebrew word halal, from which we get the word Hallelujah, which means "to praise, to be bright, to shine, to be splendid, to celebrate, to glorify, and to be famous." So can we see why the primary function of Satan in heaven was to worship? His very name means worship, and remember, he was the archangel; he led the host of the angels around the throne of God is in heaven in giving worship to God. He was dwelling constantly in the presence of God, until he was lifted up in pride and wanted to establish his throne above the throne of God. He desired this worship.

So God turned him out of heaven. According to Isaiah 14:11, "Thy pump is brought down to the grave and The noise of thy viols. How art thou fallen from heaven oh Lucifer son of the morning. How art thou cut down to the ground which didst weaken the nations, for thou said in thy heart. I will ascend into heaven. I will exalt my throne above the stars of God I will sit upon the mount of the congregation. I will ascend above the cloud I will be like the most high." Notice how many times the word *I* is mentioned in these verses. Pride was his fall, for pride goes before destruction and a haughty spirit before a fall. This is the reason God removed him from this place of worship, and he took one-third of the worshippers with him.

The Bible says he is now the god of this world. When they fell, I believe there was a void left in heaven, and God came down and lifted men up by sending His Son, Jesus Christ, to redeem us back to Himself. Through His grace and mercy, He puts us, as His chosen people, in this place of power and authority. We are saved for this main purpose, and I do believe in this present generation. There is a chosen set that is set apart for this purpose. 1 Peter 2:5 says, "Ye also are lively stones built up a spiritual houses holy priesthood to offer up spiritual sacrifice acceptable to God by Jesus Christ." Revelation 1:6 also says, "And has made us kings and priest unto our father to him be glory and Dominion for ever and ever."

Now I realize why we have so much perverted music in the world today, and I have seen people worshipping these people; bowing down, crying, passing out, even to a point where some had to be taken out on stretchers, rushing them to the ER. They will do anything to touch their favorite artist, who can only make them high for one or two hours. Sometimes they have to drug themselves to get high so that they will be able to excite the people, and they themselves are miserable and need a divine touch from the hands of God.

On the contrary, look at the difference between some of our anointed praise and worship leaders, along with their groups. Their lives are being changed and transformed; deliverance and healing will take place; breakthroughs will come. You feel refreshed. You feel like if the devil was a visible foe, you would tear him apart. But here's what the Lord said in Isaiah 42:8: "I am the Lord that is my name, and my glory will I not give to another, neither my praise to any graven image." Also, in verse 9, he said to those that are set in their traditional way of worship, "Behold the former things are come to pass, a new thing do I declare before they spring forth, I'll tell you of them. Sing unto the Lord a new song and his praise from the end of the earth."

Similarly, verses 12–13 say, "Let them give glory unto the Lord and declare his praise in the Islands. The Lord shall go forth as a mighty man, he shall stir up jealousy like a mighty man of war he shall cry yea. Roar; he shall prevail against his enemies, and let God arise on our praise and his enemies be scattered." Thank you, Jesus. He said the former way of worship came to pass. Now He is doing a new thing in our churches. Life is coming to our worship. The spirit of the Lord is moving in the body like never before, but there are deeper depths and higher heights. We can move up higher. Our hearts should be crying out for more of Him.

We are a generation of priests who are offering up spiritual sacrifices. David said he delighted not in burnt offerings, else he would give them, but he said the sacrifices of God are broken spirits. He will not despise a broken and contrite heart. Paul also said in the book of Romans 12:1, "I beseech thee therefore, brethren by the mercies of God that ye present your body as a living sacrifice holy and acceptable unto God which is our reasonable service."

In worship, we are offering ourselves to God, and it is a reasonable service. Remember, all the characters who have been mentioned in this book so far have had to do with the offering of themselves. The priest offered themselves. Adam offered himself until he fell; Isaiah offered himself; the woman at the well offered herself and encouraged others to do the same. Paul said, "I count everything but dung that I might win Christ," and so he encouraged the Roman brethren to give themselves as a sacrifice. He said, "I die daily, and I kept my body under subjection." In Romans 12:2, he went on to say, "Be not conform to this world but be transformed by the renewing of your mind." The greatest battleground is the mind of man, which, therefore, must be renewed to offer effective worship to God. "As a man thinks in his heart so is he the mind also can be used interchangeable with the heart" (Proverbs 23:7). Matthew 9:4 says, "Why think ye evil in your heart?"

The Bible also tells us to guard the heart, for out of it come the issues of life. Paul, in his final letter to the Philippians brethren, says, "Whatsoever things are true, whatsoever things are honest, whatsoever things are lovely, whatsoever things are of good report, if there be any venture, if there be any praise, think on these things." Yes, for out of the abundance of the heart the mouth speaks; as long as the mind or the heart is filled with God's Word, then worship will flow.

Psalm 106:2–3 says, "Who can utter the mighty acts of God? Who can shew forth all his praise? Blessed are they that keep judgment and he that doth righteousness at all times."

Why should we worship? David gave us some of the reasons why we should. In Psalms 103:1, David said, "Bless the Lord oh my soul." The soul consists of the mind, the emotions, and the will. Man is a triune being: body, soul, and spirit. So there was a war going on in his soul realm to keep him from worshipping the Lord. The soul is the most difficult part of us to control, and secondly, the will of man. Even Jesus had to pray to His father for His will to be submissive to the will of the Father. He stayed in the garden of Gethsemane as He prayed to His father with the weight of the sin of the world on Him. As He faced the bitter cup, He said, "Father, if it is possible, let this cup pass from me." Can you imagine the pain in His heart knowing the type of death that He was about to face? But He said nevertheless, "Let not My will but Your will be done."

The Grace Thrillers song, *Let This Same Prayer Be Mine Every Day*. So David had to rise in intercession and talk to his soul; he had to command his soul; he also declared to his soul the reason why it should bless the Lord. He said, "Bless the Lord, oh my soul. Soul, you will rise to worship, and all that is within me, bless His holy name." There are times in our lives when the cares of this world will try to keep us down. We will become depressed and discouraged, but we must rise up and declare war against the enemy. The enemy watches for our unguarded hour to launch his attack, but with intercessory worship, we can defeat him.

In 2 Chronicles 20:1, Jehoshaphat wins a battle for Israel by sending the singers, or worshippers, first ahead of the army. When he heard that the Ammonites and the Moabites' great army was coming to war against Israel, he went to seek the face of the Lord; he called all the people in the land of Judah together and proclaimed a fast. He stood in the midst of the congregation and prayed, "Oh Lord, God of our fathers, are thou not God in heaven and ruleset not Thou over all the kingdoms of the earth? In Thine hand, is there not power and might so that none is able to withstand Thee?" God, we have no power to fight against this great army; we don't know what to do, but our eyes are on You.

He prayed and prayed until the Lord spoke through the prophet Jahaziel and said, "Harken all Judah, thus saith the Lord; be not afraid nor be dismayed by reason of this great multitude. For the battle is not yours but God's. You have no need to fight in this battle. Set yourself, stand still, and see the salvation of the Lord. Fear not, for the Lord is with thee." And Jehoshaphat and Judah bowed themselves to the ground and worshipped the Lord.

They rose early in the morning, and Jehoshaphat told the people to "believe in the Lord your God, so shall ye be established. Believe His prophet so shall he prosper, and he appointed singers unto the Lord to worship the Lord in the beauty of holiness." They went out before the army and sang praise to the Lord for His mercy endured forever. When they began to sing and praise, the Lord set a holy abashment and destroyed every one of them; not one escaped. They even turned on each other, so none was able to escape the judgment of God. This is the power that is in praise and worship.

In Acts 16:25, Paul and Silas were stripped and beaten severely and put into prison for preaching the gospel of Jesus Christ, but at midnight, they started singing praises to God, and the prisoners heard, and I believe they were enjoying the worship. Suddenly, there was an earthquake that shook so hard that the prison door swung open, the bars broke off, and the chains fell off their hands and feet. Here came the prison guards, running inside, expecting all the prisoners to be gone, but the worship was so strong and the earthquake so forceful that it kept them spellbound. Now with the devastation that the guards saw and knowing the penalty for them would be certain death, they decided to take their own lives, but the apostles shouted to them, "Do thyself no harm; we are all here, but God has another plan. For all things work together for good to those that love God and are called according to His purpose."

And so the two worshippers were able to declare to them, "Do thyself no harm. we are all here." The Word of the Lord said they came bowing down before the apostles, trembling, and said, "Sir, what must I do to be saved?" When you have this great weapon in your hand, there is no need to be afraid. The enemy can be destroyed in the mighty name of Jesus. Prison bars will be broken, shackles will be loosened, and knees will bow at the lordship of Jesus Christ. Glory to God.

David continues to give reasons why we should worship Him, who forgives all thine iniquities. Can we think of how sinful some of us who were? But the mighty hand of God reaches down and lifts us up, the psalmist said, "Out of a horrible pit, out of the mired clay." But today, we are forgiven. He heals all our diseases. Sometimes the Lord heals us before we even know that we are sick. He said in His Word, "I am the Lord that healeth thee. Thank you, Jesus; he delivereth our life from destruction." There are so many destructive forces that we encounter on a daily basis. Things in the atmosphere that we see and some we cannot see with our natural eyes. The Bible says, "We are not fighting against flesh and blood, but we are fighting against principalities and powers against spiritual wickedness in high places, and as we go up to the high places of praise, we pull the devil's kingdoms down."

It is the angels that are encamping around and about us. They help us take care of those activities in the spirit realm, and they crown us with loving kindness and tender mercies. For with loving kindness, he has drawn us, and surely goodness and mercy shall follow us all the days of our lives as we dwell in His house forever. They that dwell in His house will still be praising Him. In Psalm 91:6, it says, "Thou shall not be afraid for the terror by night, nor for the pestilence that walks in darkness, nor for the destruction that wastes at noonday." He also crowns us with loving kindness and tender mercies. The Bible says, "Love is kind." When you are in love with someone, you want the very best for them; you watch over them; you protect them; and you shower them with expensive gifts to show your love and your appreciation for them. You show how grateful you are that they are a part of your life, and you will show gratitude in many different ways. We are very tender toward them. You do not want to hurt them nor do you want to see them get hurt.

Yet the love that the Lord has for us is far greater. He said in John, chapter 3, "Greater love hath no man than this that a man lay down his life for his friend." The angels of the Lord are encamped, protecting and covering those who love and fear Him. Look at Job. The Word of God says, the devil went into the presence of God and said, "I tried to tempt him, but I found out that you have an edge around him. But move the edge and he will curse you to your face," but the devil went away with his head hanging down because Job went through the permissive test with flying colors. He waited on God for his change as he continued to be a faithful worshipper. The man of integrity, Brother Job, came through the test victorious because he bore us up in his arms. Oh, glory to God. He satisfied our mouths with good things so that our youth would be renewed like the eagles. As children of God, we always look younger than our age, so many people will say to us, "You don't look your age." Oh yes, we don't. This is because of His grace and His mercies, for He beautifies the meek with salvation. If we know these things as David said and do not become forgetful hearers, worship will flow from our hearts.

I once read an article many years ago. I don't know who the writer is, and I take no credit for it, but the content blessed me, and I'll share it. It said that worship is an intimate and vital encounter with a person and their personality. True worship includes the full recognition of who God is. End of quote. A few of His attributes are that God is holy, sovereign, almighty, all-powerful, ever-loving, merciful, compassionate, and forgiving. He is omnipotent, the creator and upholder of all things. The giver and sustainer of life. Thinking of these attributes, how can we not worship Him?

I was reading a book written by A. L. and Joyce Gill, and as I was reading, the Lord put this in my spirit: a person doesn't have to be in the presence of the Lord to thank Him or to praise Him, but in worship, it is a must. The first dimension of worship is thanksgiving. Do I have to be in your presence to thank you? I don't think I have to be there. The second dimension is praise. Do I have to be in your presence to praise you? But in the third dimension, which is worship, we must be in His presence to worship. He said, "In my presence, there is a fullness of joy, and there is joy in worship. One cannot worship and remain the same, and at His right hand, which speaks of power, there are pleasures forevermore, and my worship I don't share because I am a jealous God." And the devil knew this because this was the reason for his downfall. So when Jesus was led by the Spirit into the wilderness to be tempted by the devil, he showed Jesus all the kingdoms of the world and said to Jesus, "All these things I will give to you if you just fall down and worship me." Jesus said to him, "Get thee behind Me, Satan, for it is written that thou shalt worship the Lord thy God, and Him only shalt thou serve."

After Jesus said this, the Bible says angels came and ministered to Him. Hallelujah! David said, enter His gates with thanksgiving, but we cannot remain at the gate. He also said, come into His courts with praise; come into the room; stay in the room; but there is another dimension, another level, which is worship. This takes place in the secret place of the most high; this is behind the veil, in the inner court, and this is not just a one-time visit. David in Psalm 91:1 says, "He that dwelleth in the secret place of the most high shall abide under the shadow of the almighty" (the key words here are dwell and abide). There we will have a consistent face-to-face encounter because it has to do with His person.

Praise is about Him, while worship is for Him. To offer effective worship to God, we must know. In his desperation for the Lord, Paul said, "Oh that I might know Him in the power of His resurrection and in the fellowship of His suffering." In Acts, chapter 17, the apostle Paul at Athens was waiting on Timothy and Silas to join him there. While waiting, something stirred in his spirit. He noticed that the whole city was given over to idolatry, so he went into the marketplaces and into their synagogues, preaching Christ to them. The first thing he saw was their devotion, but they were devoted to someone they did not know. Paul said, "I found an altar with the inscription: to the unknown god." They devotedly worshipped a god they did not know. They were worshipping in ignorance. They had heard of him, but they did not know him. Therefore, the image that they set up represents the god they did not know, to the unknown god.

The Word tells us not to bow down to any graven images, which is the work of men, and that He does not dwell in temples that are made with hands. It is us that He longed for that temple that was created, not made by hands. He said, "I will come in and sup with you." This way, true worship can flow through us to Him. But thanks be to God, even if we worshipped in the past in ignorance, He can forgive us. Therefore, He asks us to repent. Remember now that no number of activities for God will take the place of a heart that is right with God. King Saul offered precious sacrifices, hoping that God would overlook his disobedience. In Hosea 6:6, God said, "I desire mercy, not sacrifice, and the knowledge of God than burnt offerings." He desires not doves or pigeons, but a broken and contrite heart. God will not overlook a sinful heart; His desire is for us to devote ourselves to knowing and loving Him with all of our hearts.

Let us look at what David did in Psalm, chapter 51, when he realized that he could not worship anymore because of his sin; one who was a great worshipper. When you are called for this purpose, you cannot be comfortable not being at the place of ministry. And so he cried out, saying, "Have mercy upon me, oh God, according to thy loving kindness; do it according to the multitude of thy tender mercies; blot out my sins and my transgression. He said it is against thee, and only have I sin and done this evil in thy sight." These words were carefully chosen by David because he knew the heart of God. "The reason why I need your cleansing," he said, "Lord, is that my sin is ever before me, and you desire truth on the inward part." However, right now, my heart is not doing well. Let us be true to ourselves. Once we have the Holy Spirit in us, we know when we are not doing well. My heart is not haughty because the Holy Spirit is there to convict us of sin, and true repentance brings revival. David went on to pray: "When you deliver me, my tongue shall sing of thy righteousness, and my mouth also shall shew forth thy praise."

God does not take pleasure in our big offerings that we are able to offer without our life first being offered to Him as an offering. Then he said that God will be pleased with our offering of praise. He said, "You don't take delight in my offering if my heart is not right, but a broken and contrite heart, oh God, Thou wilt not despise." Then God will be pleased with the sacrifices of righteousness, bullocks—mature sacrifices upon the altar of the Lord. Let me ask you, the readers, the same question I ask myself: how broken are you? I ask this question because God is looking for broken spirits, so don't be so hard on yourself if you are broken.

Some of us as believers believe that when we cry, it is a sign of weakness or because we have committed some unpardonable sin, but I beg to differ. It shows strength, in my honest opinion. The word *contrite* means "to be sorry for having done wrong." It takes a strong person to acknowledge their wrongs. When God sees our willingness to repent and to turn from our sinful ways, He is pleased. He said, "My little children, I adore you that you sin not; but if you sin, you have an advocate with the Father, Jesus Christ the righteous." Why do we need to worship every day?

I was doing a corresponding course on ministry from the International School of Ministry, and one of the subjects was on praise and worship, which was done by Lamar Boschman. He said we worship because God is our Creator and He is worthy of worship. Because of His transcendent uniqueness and holiness, we need to worship. He further explained that for us to feel good, we should love God as He meant so much to us. Our hearts are pregnant with adoration, exhortation, and appreciation. End of quote. Worship becomes a love response born out of a relationship with God, and we worship to please God.

Another important part of our worship is the music and the musicians. I am praying for the day to come when all churches will grow numerically and financially so that our musicians and praise team can be employed full-time in this ministry. If we want our musicians to be effective and dedicated to this ministry, we need to treat them well and employ them as full-time workers in the church. Is this impossible? In my most humble opinion, no, it's definitely not. We can set this as a goal and work toward it. In 1 Chronicles 9:33, and these are singers, chief of the fathers of the Levites, who remaining in the chambers were free, for they were employed in that work day and night. 1 Chronicle 15:16 says, "And David spoke to the chief of the Levites to appoint brethren to be singers with instruments of music, psalteries, harps, and symbols, sounds lifting up the voice with joy."

I do believe this is one of the reasons why we are losing them to the world, and if we do keep them, they act as if they are doing the church a favor. They end up coming when they feel like it, with no consecration and no commitment. The church shouldn't do this, but I guarantee that if we fix this area of the team in our churches, we will see significant changes in them. When we truly think about it, more time will be spent on rehearsals and prayer, as the music is just as important as the singers. Also, bear in mind that we cannot just pick someone off the street and put them in this office because we are desperate. No, we must spend time getting them and knowing who they are.

Let us remember that there are spirits out there that we can't afford to let into our congregation, especially among our young people. Have we noticed how some of the megachurches are professional and dedicated? The leaders are taken care of, and there is a significant difference in their worship services. Oh, how vital and important the musicians and the music are to the church services. Listen to what Psalms 150:3 says: "Praise him with the sound of the trumpet; praise him with the psaltery and harp; praise him with the timbrel and dance. Praise him with the stringed instruments and organs; praise him upon the loud cymbals; praise him upon the high-sounding cymbals. Let everything that has breath, life, or can make a sound, praise the Lord" because we love Him. He means so much to us that our hearts are pregnant with adoration, exhortation, and appreciation. Worship becomes a love response born out of a relationship.

When you love someone, there will be times of intimacy. So let us look for a moment at the area of intimacy between a husband and his wife. During this time, the first thing that most persons do is be alone with their spouse. Behind closed doors, this is a time when you do not want to be disturbed. Once alone, then comes the time for foreplay: the kisses, caresses, and all the nice words to arouse your lover. During this time, you would never want your spouse to talk about the bills not being paid. Even topics about the family, as important as they are, you don't want to talk about them, the neighbors' mother, father, sisters, or brothers. This is just not the time for that. Even before you go in that bedroom or behind closed doors, we start with that loving gaze, the touches, the kind words, the hugs, and love songs; yes, love songs. There are many clean love songs that we can sing to our spouses.

Have you ever read the book of Solomon? This is the love between Christ and His church. Maybe if we knew this, we would not be so afraid of this book, even to preach about it. Let us also bear in mind that lovemaking does not start in the bedroom. It is the overflow of two lovers' attitudes and behaviors throughout the day toward each other. So if the couple does not have a good relationship with each other throughout the day, there is no way that intimacy can be as enjoyable as it was meant to be. Even so with the Lord, as it is in the natural, so it is in the spiritual. There must be constant fellowship and intimacy with the Lord so that our worship will flow on Sunday morning. We can't be miserable on the job and at home from Monday to Saturday, and then come on Sunday morning to have a Hallelujah time and to lead the church into where you have not been all week.

Some years ago, someone who knows how much I love praise and worship gave me a few notes on worship. He said, in some ways, worship defies definition. It can only be experienced, but like every experience in life, we need to give it a definition to help us understand the experience and to enter into it more wholeheartedly. Therefore, the writer has this to say that the English word for worship comes from an old Anglo-Saxon word, *worth ship*. It is a recognition of and a response to the worth of God. When we value the worth of someone, we usually do something to demonstrate their worth. Psalm 96:8 states that we should ascribe to the Lord glory and strength; ascribe unto the Lord the glory due unto His name; make His praise glorious. Worship is the human response to the perceived presence of the divine. A presence that transcends normal human activities and is holy.

The holy presence of God penetrates our ordinary space in such a way that it arouses human awareness. The sacred and the profane are united, not just united but reunited, because this is the whole purpose of God creating us to be in this place of worship and communication with Him. It is both an attitude and an act. Why do we worship? We worship Him because He is most worthy (2 Chronicles 16:23). Sing unto the Lord, all the earth shews forth his praise from day to day, not just Sunday morning or on the Sabbath day. But from day to day, it is supposed to be a continuous shewing forth of His salvation, declare His glory among the heathen, His marvelous works among all nations. For great is the Lord and greatly to be praised. He also is to be feared above all gods, for all the gods of the earth are idols. They are made with silver and gold; they are the works of men; they are man-made, but the Lord made the heavens.

The psalmist said in Psalms 19:1, "The heaven declare the glory of God and His firmament showed His handiworks, day-to-day uttered speech, night unto night, showing the knowledge of our God. Among the gods there is none like Him neither are any works like Thy works; all nations, whom Thou hast made shall come and worship before Thee and glorify Thee." He is calling on every nation and tongue to worship, for the Lord is a great God and a great King. Because the earth is His, the sea is His, and He made it. Righteousness and judgment are the foundations of His throne. Psalm 148:3 says, "Praise ye Him, sun and moon; praise Him all ye stars of light; praise Him, ye heavens of heaven and ye waters that be above the heavens. Let them praise the Lord, for He commanded, and they were created. He has also established them forever." Have we noticed that the stars cannot go out, neither the sun nor the moon? They will continue to shine as long as this world lasts. These are a few of the reasons why we praise our God. We sing to Him in the congregation of the righteous; we sing about Him to the heathen and make His glory known. Even if we don't, the heavens declare His glory. They are declaring the wonders of our God.

Were you able to wake up this morning and breathe in some fresh air? That's God. Psalm 34:2 says, "My soul make her boast in the Lord; the humble shall hear thereof and be glad." Psalms 149 says, "Let Israel rejoice in Him that made Him; let the children of Zion be joyful in their King. Let them praise His name in the dance; let them sing praises unto Him with the timbrel and harp." Some people feel like some of our churches, such as mine, make too much noise. What do the Scriptures have to say to support noise in churches? In Psalms

81:1, it says, "Sing aloud unto God our strength makes a joyful noise unto the God of Jacob." It also says in 95:1, "Come let us sing unto the Lord; let us make a joyful noise to the rock of our salvation," and let us remember that around the throne of God, according to the Scriptures. Thousands of angels are singing, and the saints will be joining in the worship throughout eternity. In hell, there will be weeping and wailing and gnashing of teeth, so both places will be noisy. So let us practice while we are still here; get used to the noise. We are just practicing here. Throughout the Scriptures, I notice any time someone comes into contact with Jesus, there is always an unusual reaction. The woman with the issues of blood touches Jesus's garment, and her issues dry up. Jesus asked, "Who touched me?" She came trembling. The woman at the well ran into her village and said, "Come see a man."

When Mary Magdalene saw Him after His resurrection in His glorified body, she could not keep it to herself. She ran into the village and told the disciples that He had risen. Evil spirits can also flee from the presence of anointed music. The Bible tells us in Samuel 16:14 that the spirit of the Lord departed from Saul and an evil spirit from the Lord was upon him, and one of his servants said to him, "Let me go seek out a man who is a cunning player upon the harp. It shall come to pass when the evil spirit from the Lord is upon thee that he shall play with his hand and thou shalt be well." So the saying pleased Saul, and he said, "Find me such a man and bring him to me." Immediately, another one of his servants said, "I know one of Jesse's sons that is cunning in playing, and he is a mighty valiant man and a man of war."

Prudent in matters, a comely person, and the Lord is with him, David the psalmist was chosen for this task, and when he came before Saul, the Word said he loved him greatly. His father was asked by Saul if he would allow him to be his armor-bearer, and it came to pass when the evil spirit of the Lord was upon Saul. Then David would play his harp, and the evil spirit would depart. Saul was refreshed. I now know that this is what will happen when anointed people play anointed instruments. Healing takes place, and David was more than qualified for this great job. But the most important person in all of this is the Holy Spirit, and the Holy Spirit was upon David. The

Holy Spirit was upon the instrument, and it drove the evil spirit from Saul, and by the grace of God, we can still find players with these qualifications today. Yes, the spirit of the Lord is upon this present generation to do exploits for God.

Just magnify the Lord with me, and let us exalt His name together. Listen to what Psalm 39:2 says: "I was dumb with silence; I held my peace, even from God, and my sorrow was stirred. Then my heart was hot within me, but while I was musing, the fire burned, then spoke I with my tongue." When we become silent and refrain from praising the Lord, our problems will remain, but praise brings release in the realm of the spirit. When David started musing on the Word again, he said the fire burned, and then he started worshipping once more.

Psalm 51:15 says, "Open thou my lips and my mouth shall shew forth Thy praise." Psalm 40:5 similarly highlighted: "Many, oh Lord, are Thy wonderful works which Thou have done, they cannot be recon up in order unto Thee." There are many more verses that can be mentioned, specifically about the goodness of God. Verse 10 explains, "I have not concealed Thy loving kindness and Thy truth from the great congregation." That is why it is necessary to have special testimony services in our churches so that God's people can talk of His goodness. This too motivates worship. This was a very special service in the past, but now we refer to testimonial services as being old-fashioned. We tend not to do it in our services anymore, or it is done once a year. But how are we making it known in the great congregation?

Oh, let us sing unto the Lord and make a joyful noise unto the rock of our salvation. And I will end with the words of this song. I'm not sure who the writer is, so I take no credit for it, but it always blesses my heart, and the words are, "Stand up, stand up for Jesus, ye shoulders of the cross, lift high His royal banner, ye must not suffer loss from victory unto victory, His army shall He lead, till every foe is vanquished, and Christ is Lord indeed. Stand up, stand up for Jesus, the strife will not be long. This day the noise of battle, the next the victory song." Is there a battle that you are facing today? If yes, then start singing.

The wise man Solomon said, "A merry heart doeth good like a medicine." He further exclaims that the Lord loves a cheerful giver, even in our giving to the Lord the glory due unto His name and making His praise glorious. We are supposed to do it cheerfully. Christians are supposed to be the happiest people on earth because we have Him who makes us happy. The Holy Spirit, listen to what Jesus calls Him, the comforter, and He said He will not speak of Himself. He is representing the Lord Jesus Christ. One of the most popular songs that we sing during the Christmas holiday, which everybody enjoys, is "Joy to the World." This is the most joyous time of the year on the planet, and even those that don't even believe in Him celebrate and enjoy the season. There is something about the name *Jesus*. Let us make His praises glorious.

About the Author

Reverend Venetta Bloomfield is originally from a small town in Trelawny, Jamaica. After relocating to Kingston, Jamaica, she was saved in 1972 under Bishop V. T. Williams's ministry. She then attended the Evangelistic School of Ministry in 1979. In that very same year, she was asked to co-pastor a young congregation in St. Mary, Jamaica. In 1993, she was called to full-time ministry with the Faith Assembly Ministries Inc. Int'l (FAMII) in Mandeville, Manchester, and then attended and graduated from the Ebenezer Bible Institute in 1995 with her bachelor's in biblical theology. She was then ordained as a minister in 1998. During her fifteen-year tenure with FAMII, she pastored four branches of the church, all located in Manchester. In 2006, just before migrating to the US, she graduated from Vision International University with another associate's degree in biblical theology and studies. From 2007 to 2012, she was the assistant pastor of the Fountain of Faith Ministries located in Baltimore, Maryland. She currently serves as the associate pastor of Baltimore Central New Testament Church of God.

www.ingramcontent.com/pod-product-compliance
Lightning Source LLC
Chambersburg PA
CBHW021814150726

47989CB00004B/1924